Dear Jerri

Everytime I see anything
about gardening I think
about you (and my sweet
grandmother). Both of
you could make anything
grow.

Thanks for being such a
faithful friend.

God Bless You.
Dee

In My
Garden

In My
Garden

written and illustrated by

A. CORT SINNES

**Andrews McMeel
Publishing**
Kansas City

ISBN: 0-7407-4205-1

Library of Congress Control Number: 2003113021

04 05 06 07 08 WKT 10 9 8 7 6 5 4 3 2 1

Book design and composition by
Kelly & Company, Lee's Summit, Missouri

ATTENTION: SCHOOLS AND BUSINESSES

Andrews McMeel books are available at quantity
discounts with bulk purchase for educational, business,
or sales promotional use. For information, please write to:
Special Sales Department, Andrews McMeel Publishing,
4520 Main Street, Kansas City, Missouri 64111.

For the two Scotts

Who else would be so happy to see you
they pee on the floor?

*Working in the garden . . . gives
me a profound feeling of inner peace.
Nothing here is in a hurry. There is no
rush toward accomplishment, no blowing
of trumpets. Here is the great mystery of
life and growth. Everything is changing,
growing, aiming at something, but
silently, unboastfully, taking its time.*

Ruth Stout (1885–1980)

Introduction

IT WAS A DARK AND STORMY NIGHT, in the middle of winter. I sat bolt upright in bed and said the words "I don't do dark and cold well" out loud. It was 3:30 in the morning.

Was I dreaming about a tropical island? Having a flashback to an Ingmar Bergman film? No, I was dreaming it was summer and that I got to spend time in my garden again. In the warmth . . . in the sun.

I pulled on some clothes, went downstairs to my office, and wrote the following story with only the computer screen for light. "I don't do dark and cold well" were the first words I wrote. By six in the morning, the story was done. I went back to bed. When I awoke again, I barely remembered having written it. Since then I haven't changed a word. So I guess you could say *In My Garden* was kind of a gift from some sleepy place that managed its way out, into the light of day. Unbidden. Unexpected. Like a volunteer seedling that appears from nowhere, only to surprise and delight as it comes into bloom.

I was born in California and from the very beginning was attracted to the outdoors. Warm sunshine, and all that grows in its presence, was imprinted on my soul at a very early age. In my adult life I spent seven years living in the Midwest. As much as I loved it, I would dream about walking barefoot on sun-warmed tiles, being surrounded by green, nurtured by a benign climate. Ultimately it became imperative to return to where I first tasted water and felt the kiss of the sun.

This story is my way of saying thanks . . . thanks for being able to grow where I was first planted.

In My
Garden

I don't do
dark and cold well.

Like a Scandinavian lizard,
I must be cold-blooded
and crave the light, doing
push-ups on a morning
sun-warmed rock.

In kindergarten
I pushed the miracle
of nasturtium seeds into
an empty milk carton
filled with soil.

I've never been
the same since.

I wonder where the
lizard spends the winter?
I know we both wait
impatiently for
spring to return.

Voltaire wrote
*"Cela est bien dit, repondit Candide,
mais il faut cultiver notre jardin."*
("That is well said, replied Candide,
but we must cultivate our garden.")

Crosby, Stills, and Nash wrote
*". . . and we've got to get
ourselves back to the garden."*

I couldn't agree more.

I have two friends
I garden with,
Scout and Spot.

Even I get their names
mixed up, so I call
them both Scott.

One name for two dogs.

When the peep-peep birds
announce morning's almost
here, I pull on my favorite
three articles of clothing:
a pair of gym shorts
and two deck shoes,
one left and one right.

Me, the lizard, and the Scotts make our way into the garden to survey the situation.

We find a patch of sun and see what has to be done.

I like weeds because they are so obvious and simple. are so obvious and simple.

They just sit there waiting to be pulled.

Pulling weeds is a satisfying
way to enter the day.

I recite my mantra of
National Public Radio reporters:

"Maria Hinojosa . . . Snigha Prakash
. . . Mandalit del Barco . . .
Sylvia Poggioli . . ."

pronouncing each one
slowly and correctly.

An old man once said
that the surest way to stay
in shape was to work up
a sweat every day.

By early afternoon,
even the lizard has retreated
and the Scotts lounge on the
cool soil under the acanthus.

From the top of the oak tree
the cicadas broadcast the
weather report: HOT.

HOT... HOT ...HOT...
... HOT... ...HOT
HOT... HOT ...
... HOT
...HOT
HOT...
HOT...
...
...HOT
HOT... ..HOT...
... HOT ... HOT... HOT
HOT... HOT... HOT...
... HOT... HOT... HOT

The Mediterraneans have it right: The middle of the day is made for a nap.

A gentle wind rises off the valley floor and stirs the tops of the ancient fir trees.

The turkey vultures make lazy circles in the sky.

The hammock is a perfect invention.

Plant a lot of plants.

That way there will always
be something new to see.

And something that
needs to be done.

Propping up an
excited tomato who's
outgrown its cage.

Getting dizzy from
a rose who has so much
fragrance it can't contain
it anymore.

Using my thumb and forefinger to thwart the natural desires of the basil plants:

It wants to flower.

I want my spaghetti al pesto.

Explaining to the
nasturtiums that they
simply cannot have all
of the gravel path.

A friend of mine once remarked, "It occurs to me that you have a lot of living things to take care of . . ."

Yes, but they also take care of me.

The hoe is a useful tool.

Any toxins—real or imagined—
drain easily through the handle
and into the soil, where they
quietly disappear.

The Scotts are partial
to the tennis ball plant.
It's a prolific thing.

I try to throw them away,
but they always come back.

"You've got mail."
Is that the telephone
I hear ringing?

The world can wait.

This is the world.

When it finally cools down the Scotts want fresh fruit from the tennis ball plant. They want me to throw it away, throw it away, throw it away.

When they've finally had their fill, they put their paws in the fountain and gulp with abandon.

Freddy Flame-Out is a friend of mine. He's a rufous hummingbird with a penchant for speed and great heights. First he saddles up next to me just to make sure I'm watching. Next thing he's taken the invisible elevator to the umpteenth sky floor, disappearing from view. Next thing I know, he's back, screeching and smoking to a stop, right next to my ear.

Freddy's an amusing friend.

There was an old stump
in my garden

whose arteries had begun
to harden

but I kept it around

as a place for woodpeckers
to pound

who are grateful
I gave it a pardon.

High summer, with its
long days folding and
unfolding upon each
other, one after another.
A time to revel in sheer
joy of being alive.

One day lengthens
into another
until they begin
to become shorter.

Under the ancient
Gravenstein apple tree,
the air smells like cider,
and wasps search madly
for ripe fruit.

The biggest, heaviest tomatoes of the year lurk deep within a dark cave of foliage, treasures of the season.

Pumpkins begin
their migration from
green to gold.

Sensing the change in the seasons, the crickets and cicadas begin a frenzied song. I think the lyric goes like this: "I'll be lost if I don't find a date before frost. Don't make me wait another year to mate. I'll be lost if I don't find a date before frost."

The early evening shadows creep up the hill. When the sun is almost done with its work for the day, the Scotts and I head for the Sunset Bench.

One of the Scotts scratches his back on the pine needles and cones, paws in the air. The other Scott sits witness with me. I think we say the same prayer to the sun:

Thank you.

Hope to see you tomorrow.

The End